Zacchaeus & the Happy Day

RHONDA GOWLER GREENE

PICTURES BY
SANTIAGO COHEN

zonderkidz

zonderkidz
The children's group
of Zondervan

www.zonderkidz.com

Requests for information should be addressed to:
Grand Rapids, Michigan 49530

Library of Congress Cataloging-in-Publication Data

Greene, Rhonda Gowler.
    Zacchaeus & the happy day / by Rhonda Gowler Greene ; illustrated
by Santiago Cohen.
        p. cm.
    ISBN-13: 978-0-310-71100-1 (printed hardcover)
    ISBN-10: 0-310-71100-2 (printed hardcover)
    1. Zacchaeus (Biblical figure)-Juvenile literature. I. Cohen, Santiago. II.
Title. III. Title: Zacchaeus and the happy day.
    BS2520.Z3G75 2007
    226.4'09505–dc22
                                                2006034426

Editor: Bruce Nuffer
Art direction and Design: Al Cetta

Printed in China

07 08 09 10 11 • 10 9 8 7 6 5 4 3 2 1

A man was there by the name of Zacchaeus;
he was a chief tax collector and was wealthy.
He wanted to see who Jesus was, but being a short man he could not, because of the crowd.
Taken from Luke 19:2-3

For my son, Aaron, with love—RGG

For my nephews, and their return—SC

One day Jesus
came to town.
People gathered
all around.

Mommies, daddies,
girls and boys.
Such a crowd! Such a noise!

Everyone had
come to see
the special man
from Galilee.

Step, step
Was that him
coming, coming,
round the bend?

The tax collector
of the town,
Zacchaeus, known for miles around

for being greedy
and unfair,
for taking much more than his share,

stood in the crowd.
But he was small.
He couldn't see a thing at all.

He tried to find
the perfect spot
where he could see. But he could not.

He tried this way,
that way too.
What could small Zacchaeus do?

Oh, how he wished
that he could see.
Then he spied—

a sycamore tree!

And so Zacchaeus
climbed and climbed.
Hurry, hurry,
not much time!

Up that tree
with branches tall—
the perfect spot for one so small.

Now above
the crowd below,
sitting high in
Jericho,

Zacchaeus perched
up in that tree,
oh, so glad that he could see.

And there was Jesus
walking past.
Yes, he saw him then at last!

Step, stop!
Oh, my! Right then—
Jesus looked up straight at him!

"Zaccheus,"
he heard Jesus say.
"I must come to your
house today."

Surprised, Zacchaeus hurried down!
He led Jesus through the town.

Step step
They made their way
to his house that happy day,

though people murmured,
"Why choose him?
A man whose heart is full of sin?"

But—oh, what joy
when Jesus came.
Salvation filled that home, not blame.

Yes, love, abundant,
filled that place.
Zacchaeus felt it…

felt God's grace.

Zacchaeus then
did something good,
something that he knew he should.

His greedy heart
grew BIG that day.
He said, "I gladly will repay

money I took
from the poor—
all I took and even more."

kind and giving in God's sight.